GOOD FRIDAY'S GOOD NEWS

GOOD FRIDAY'S GOOD NEWS

Meditations for the Mean Meantime

Eric W. Gritsch

EDITED BY
Bonnie A. Brobst
and Elizabeth A. Yates

FOREWORD BY
Theodore F. Schneider

ILLUSTRATED BY
Othmar Carli

CASCADE *Books* · Eugene, Oregon

GOOD FRIDAY'S GOOD NEWS
Meditations for the Mean Meantime

Cascade Books
An Imprint of Wipf and Stock Publishers
199 W. 8th Ave., Suite 3
Eugene, OR 97401
www.wipfandstock.com

ISBN 13: 978-1-62564-566-1

Cataloging-in-Publication data:

Gritsch, Eric W.

Good Friday's good news : meditations for the mean meantime
/ edited by Bonnie A. Brobst and Elizabeth A. Yates, illustrated by
Othmar Carli, with a foreword by Theodore F. Schneider.

xxii + 52 p.; 23 cm.

ISBN 13: 978-1-62564-566-1

1. Evangelical Lutheran Church in America—Sermons. 2. Lutheran Church—Sermons. 3. Lenten sermons. I. Brobst, Bonnie A. II.
Schneider, Theodore F., 1934– III. Cali, Othmar. IV. Title.

BV4277 G757 2014

Manufactured in the USA

CONTENTS

Sermons by The Reverend Dr. Eric W. Gritsch
Delivered during Good Friday Worship
St. Matthew Lutheran Church, York, Pennsylvania
April 9, 1993, Noon

The Seven Last Words of Jesus from the Cross

LIST OF ILLUSTRATIONS

FOREWORD

After a long day and a welcome dinner, I settled into my comfortable chair in Jerusalem and found on my tablet the manuscript of these seven Good Friday homilies by my late friend, teacher, and colleague, Eric W. Gritsch. I felt much too weary to start reading. "I shall be asleep for sure in five minutes," I thought. Such had been the series of days in Jerusalem. "But, why not have just a taste?" And, I did!

I could not put it down! It was as if one were hearing Eric Gritsch in person. His grasp of human history and Christian theology, along with surprising insights laced often with good-natured humor, for which he is known to students and colleagues alike worldwide, were right here, on the page.

It is not often that spoken words can be transcribed into written text and yet have their spontaneity and humor, surprise and sparkle. Spoken words are enhanced by vocal inflexions, expressions, and gestures. One would not expect such things in a transcribed text. Perhaps they are imagined, but for those who knew him and surely for others, the sparkle, surprises, and appropriate humor are all here!

From the opening homily of this Good Friday series, the Reverend Dr. Gritsch has our full attention: "On this day, at about this hour, Dietrich Bonhoeffer was hanged by the Nazis and burned so that nothing was left." Here begins the history of another execution of one believed to be a prophet in our era. Then come the words from the cross: "Father, forgive them; for they know not what they do." Dr. Gritsch then asks, "I wonder if the Nazis knew what they were doing . . . ?"

Then he was on to his theme. Christians are all about forgiveness, or ought to be, as was our Lord. The homily developed, touching Scripture, history, theology, and the experience of our own living together in Christ.

Well, I was hooked! On I read, no longer the least bit drowsy, but rather hungry to hear, to learn, or perhaps just to see what this great historian, theologian, writer, teacher, preacher, and colleague of so many of us in the life of the Church would do to exegete these precious seven words of our Lord. I would not be disappointed. I read five of the seven homilies that evening. I have reread these seven homilies again and again since.

He was a profound preacher and teacher, a lecturer in high demand in the United States and Europe even after his retirement following thirty years on the faculty of the Lutheran Theological Seminary at Gettysburg. Anecdotal stories, both humorous and insightful, are yet apprecia-tively told on that campus.

Dr. Gritsch was a prolific writer, with one or two manuscripts in process on his desk right up to the last, when surprisingly his desk was clear for the first time. He appeared to have a quiet and confident understanding of the meaning of his time.

His spiritual life and piety were rooted in every ex-pression of the church—from his active congregational involvement to his work on many fronts with his synod to his service on dialogue committees and task forces of the Evangelical Lutheran Church in America. He was known to be able to untangle, with solid scriptural footing and with logic, some of the thorniest issues for the church in our time. His insight would be marked always with contemporary relevance, and always ecumenical in its vision.

If you knew Eric W. Gritsch, here is an opportunity to hear and experience him again as we wait together for that day when we shall be "together with our Lord." (1 Thess. 4:17)

If readers are meeting Eric W. Gritsch for the first time in this little book of seven homilies on our Lord's words from the cross, I suggest this book will inspire, teach, engage, surprise, and even cause a smile now and again at how it is that this great teacher can draw us into his own conversation and contemplation into Him who was the "Word [who] became flesh and dwelt among us, full of grace and truth, whose glory we have beheld as the only Son from the Father." (John 1:14, RSV)

In both cases, this little book will hold a special place on our library shelves or even on the prayer desk or other places of our study and meditation. It already has these places for me. Moreover, I shall gift it to my friends.

The Rev. Dr. Theodore F. Schneider, Bishop Emeritus
The Metropolitan Washington DC Synod, ELCA

PREFACE

The text was transcribed from sermons delivered by Dr. Eric W. Gritsch at St. Matthew Lutheran Church, York, Pennsylvania, on Good Friday, April 9, 1993. The recordings were transcribed verbatim by Elizabeth Yates. This text was then edited by both Bonnie Brobst and Liz Yates. Together, by reading and listening, the sermons were edited for clarity and style. The final agreed-upon text intends to be faithful to the spoken words of Dr. Gritsch.

Dr. Gritsch's quotes are often paraphrases of the words of speakers or texts so are not footnoted.

The titles of the Last Words of Jesus are taken from the New Revised Standard Version (NRSV). The words used by Dr. Gritsch in the sermons are sometimes from the NRSV and sometimes from the King James Version (KJV).

The coeditors and illustrator have made this project a labor of love. All proceeds from this book will be used to memorialize Eric W. Gritsch.

Anyone wishing to obtain a copy of the audio version of Dr. Gritsch's sermons printed as *Good Friday's Good News* is invited to go to www.ericwgritsch.org for information regarding the ordering of the CD. This website

provides information pertaining to the life and work of Eric
W. Gritsch as well as a complete listing of his books.

Holy Cross Day, September 14, 2013

B.A.B.

E.A.Y.

CONTRIBUTORS

Author and Preacher

Eric W. Gritsch (1931–2012)

- Emeritus Professor of Church History, Lutheran Theological Seminary Gettysburg

- Native of Austria

- Experienced the reign of Adolf Hitler and Russian military occupation

- Ordained: Evangelical Lutheran Church in America

- Educated: University of Vienna, University of Zurich, University of Basel, Yale Divinity School at Yale University

- Fulbright Scholar

- Director of Institute of Luther Studies at Gettysburg

- Delegated Participant in U.S. Lutheran–Catholic Dialogue (1971–1992)

- Taught at Wellesley College, Gettysburg Lutheran Seminary (1961–1994), Catholic University of America, California Lutheran University, Ecumenical Institute at St. Mary's Seminary and University (Baltimore, MD)

- Authored twenty-five books, including
  Martin—God's Court Jester (1983)
  Fortress Introduction to Lutheranism (1994)
  The Wit of Martin Luther (2006)
  Toxic Spirituality (2009)
  A History of Lutheranism (2nd rev. ed., 2010)
  Martin Luther's Anti-Semitism (2012)
  Christendumb (2013)
  Numerous essays, reviews, and translations

- Frequent teacher and preacher in the church at large

- Married to Bonnie A. Brobst

Coeditors

Bonnie Ann Brobst, Baltimore, Maryland

- Widow of the late Eric W. Gritsch

- Education Director of the Chesapeake Alternative School in Baltimore, MD, a secondary facility for at-risk youth

- Member of Zion Church of the City of Baltimore, Baltimore, MD

Elizabeth Anne Yates, Richmond, VA

- MDiv, Union Theological Seminary, Richmond, Virginia

- Lutheran Year at Lutheran Theological Seminary, Gettysburg, Pennsylvania

- Ordained: Evangelical Lutheran Church in America

- Student and friend of Eric Gritsch

- Member of Christ the King Lutheran Church, Richmond, VA

Illustrator

Othmar Carli, Painter/Sculptor, York, PA

- Longtime friend of Eric W. Gritsch

- Native of Austria

- Commissioned by CRUTA, The Foundation for Conservation & Research of Urban Traditional Architecture, for his repair and restoration of the Mahtab Trust's temple complex & palaces in Burdwan, West Bengal

- Honored by the Friends of the United Nations in 1995 for his restoration in the northern quarter of Calcutta, India, where he taught local artisans preservation techniques

- Commissioned by the Archdiocese of Vienna, Austria

- The Pennsylvania Historical & Museum Commission Gettysburg Ceremonial Courtroom 1860

- Professor of Art Technology, The Pennsylvania State University

INTRODUCTION

What a joy it was for me to hear the voice of my dear husband, Eric W. Gritsch, coming from the CD six months
after his death! In my opinion, one of Eric's gifts was to
make complex theological concepts understandable for the
average person. He was able to light a spark in the mind of
the lifelong church attendee as well as in the person who
called him- or herself a nonbeliever!

With this collection of Good Friday meditations based
upon the Seven Last Words of Christ people are able to not
only read the text but also listen to Dr. Gritsch delivering
the meditations from the pulpit of St. Matthew Lutheran
Church in York, Pennsylvania, in 1993. Those who had the
privilege of knowing this beloved and respected teacher
and scholar will recall that he rarely wrote a sermon. He
preached from key words on a three-by-five-inch index
card. Pastor Elizabeth (Liz) Yates, a former Gritsch student,
informed me that she had found these tapes in her collection and volunteered to transcribe them from the voice to
print. I was thrilled!

A sermon heard is much different than a sermon read.
I was aware, after seventeen years of marriage to this man,
and proofreading his numerous books and published ar-
ticles, that he would now want me to once again attempt to
make his thoughts as clear as possible to his readers. After
working from the transcript and his voice, Liz and I believe

that we have a written version of his sermons that would meet with Eric's approval.

Preceding each sermon is an artistic piece by Othmar Carli that may focus readers or listeners for a period of meditation and devotion. Following each sermon is a short series of questions, which could be discussion starters for study groups. However this little book is used, readers will recall Dr. Gritsch reminding us of Luther's words: "Worship and education are the twin pillars of the church." Through his simple, straightforward stories and his words, whether spoken or written, we will hear the voice of Eric W. Gritsch and benefit from his theological insights.

I am grateful to my friends who gave generously of their time and talents making this little book a gift that will keep the message of Eric W. Gritsch alive for all of us who read and study his words. My heartfelt thanks go to Liz Yates, who diligently transcribed Eric's words to print from the audiotape; Othmar Carli, who, after suffering a stroke, laboriously developed drawings with his left hand, which may lead readers to thoughtful meditation; Raymond Ridenour, who with technical expertise in the realm of visual art, formatted the drawings for print; and Ted Schneider, who lovingly wrote a foreword that captures the essence of my late husband's ministry.

Bonnie Ann Brobst, coeditor
Baltimore, Maryland

The Rev. Dr. Pr. Eric Walter Gritsch was commended to Almighty God on March 2, 2013, at Zion Church of the City of Baltimore. Colleagues, students, friends, and family gathered from around the world to honor and celebrate Dr. Gritsch's life, which showed us the way not only of servanthood but also "serpenthood" (Matt 10:16). After attending this memorial service, I returned home to find the tape recordings of his Good Friday sermons from 1993.

It was the tradition of St. Matthew Lutheran Church in York, Pennsylvania, to invite a professor from Lutheran Theological Seminary Gettysburg to preach on "The Seven Last Words of Jesus from the Cross" every Good Friday. Dr. Eric W. Gritsch was the invited preacher in 1993 when I served St. Matthew as pastoral intern.

During Holy Week (March 24–31, 2013), I experienced the sermons again while transcribing them. They give powerful witness to Good Friday's Good News in the proclamation of Pastor Gritsch, the Christian vocation most deeply etched into his heart. Dr. Gritsch wove the words of Jesus and the cloud of witnesses through his faith and remarkable life into a complete Christian theology. Those who heard Eric Gritsch the preacher remember there was no text, only three-by-five cards with a few points and quotes. Fortunately St. Matthew's recordings preserve these moving homilies for us.

This book is a labor of love, which will contribute to a memorial for Eric Walter Gritsch. I extend my deep gratitude to Eric Gritsch's widow, Bonnie Brobst, for her encouragement to pursue this project, her editing expertise, her Reflections pages in this volume, and her friendship. I offer God's grace to you as proclaimed by Eric W. Gritsch—*Good Friday's Good News* on the way to Easter. May this volume be Good News for us all as we seek to live cruciform lives of servanthood and serpenthood. *Soli Deo Gloria.*

The Rev. Elizabeth Anne Yates, coeditor
Richmond, Virginia

THE FIRST WORD

*"Father, forgive them; for they do not
know what they are doing."*

—Luke 23:34

On April 9, 1945, about this time of day, a German Lutheran pastor named Dietrich Bonhoeffer was executed by Adolf Hitler's secret police; it happened in a concentration camp in Bavaria at Flossenbürg. He was hanged and burned with gasoline with four others. So there was nothing left.

Did the Germans know what they were doing to a pastor like Bonhoeffer? Did he know what he was doing when he opposed Hitler? Did the crowd around the Cross of Jesus know what they were doing when they executed Him? We might never know. Jesus said, "Forgive them, for they do not know what they do."

Forgiveness is at the bottom line of the entire Christian faith. It is not love. It is not even faith. It is forgiveness. Before Jesus died, He told the story about Mary Magdalene and the experience with people like her. And He said at the end to the Pharisees, "Those who forgive little, love little." Forgiveness is the bottom line. And ever since Jesus died, we live by forgiveness. This is our business as Christians, and it is a very hard business, because sometimes we do know what they do to us, and therefore we do not want to forgive. Rarely do we "not know what they do." And therefore we should forgive.

It is very difficult to be that kind of Christian who lives in this new era with God where a new future has begun, where we are baptized into a new life, into an adventure with God that goes beyond the usual boundaries of this world and its moral and its cultural and its political—even its religious—sense. Jesus goes beyond that, and occasionally—occasionally—people like Dietrich Bonhoeffer cross the boundary line because the times are so tough and so confusing. Bonhoeffer decided to participate in the assassination of Adolf Hitler. That is a rare decision for an ordained Lutheran German pastor to make, and many people criticized him for it. But he felt he had to do this, and he used one word—that Christianity is "beyond religion!" There is a "religionless Christianity" if religion means just to be good and just to believe and just to be decent sometimes. Obedience to Christ goes beyond all that or is above or below all that. So Bonhoeffer wrote in a book called *Ethics*—quote: "Christian ethics is not a matter of right or wrong. It is a matter of obedience."

It is a very radical statement for Christians to make when they are to love their neighbors. And in baptism we are invited into that kind of life where the future has begun. What do we do in baptism? We undertake three steps to follow this Jesus. The first step is to say *no* to things—"Do you renounce evil and the devil and all his works?" That is the first step—to say *no*. The first step is not to say *yes* to Jesus; the first step is to get rid of some addiction, of some illusion, of something that bothers us, something that prevents us from following Jesus. The Christian *no* to some things is the first step of baptism. It used to be called exorcism—to get rid of some addiction, to drive out the confusion from one's life, to drive out evil which means confusion. (The word *diabolical* means "to be thrown about, to be confused.")

The first step is to get clarity and mission and discipleship into one's life. Then comes the second step: to confess that God is in charge, as Creator. He redeems us from sin through Jesus Christ and gives us the Holy Spirit in order to survive. That is when we say *yes* to that God of the Trinity. Together with the Church—in public—we say *yes* to follow a centuries-old tradition of first saying *no* and then saying *yes*! And then a gift is given. If you remember, when baptisms are performed—what does the pastor or those who baptize say? "You are now sealed with the Holy Spirit and marked with the Cross of Christ forever." We are sealed like a closed envelope. The Spirit is given, and whenever the Spirit decides to empower us, to give us power to live, then we do live as Christians.

Sometimes it takes a long time for the Spirit to act. Mr. Gorbachev, of late Russian fame, was baptized, communed, and confirmed as a baby in the Russian Orthodox Church near Moscow. For fifty-eight years he was a Communist who denied God. The Spirit remained sealed in that envelope of his life. And then when he was fifty-nine, he said a word that changed the world. He said *perestroika*—something like "freedom"—and Communism began to die. I think the Holy Spirit broke open the seal to make Communism go away by acting powerfully on Mr. Gorbachev. He had to say no then and live by the Christian faith and endure the power of the Holy Spirit.

That is why Martin Luther says that Good Friday is the greatest holiday of Christendom, because at that precise day, at that precise hour, at Golgotha—the place called The Skull—the entire world changed. That is what we really celebrate. That is what we really remember: that pinpointed action of God where He says, "I bear the entire sin of the world. I will give you a new future. I will give you an adventure that goes beyond death into a never-ending relationship with Me, your God. The first commandment is now valid: I am your God; you have no longer any other gods. From now on your life is linked to Mine, because I have virtually loved you to death on a Cross. It is unconditional!"

That is why Luther coined the phrase *Good Friday*. It is no longer *Karfreitag* (the woeful Friday, the painful Friday) but the Good Friday, the good day that we have, and the day of thanksgiving. That is why Good Friday liberates through the Cross. A human being (one of us) named Jesus, went on before us and stepped across that big boundary line called death. He liberated Himself and us from all the problems of this world. Ever since then we are initiated into that struggle against the old and for the new. Luther says in his *Catechism*, "Daily, daily, you must drown the old Adam, and daily you must drown the old Eve, so that the new life can rise up and dominate you from now on."

I remember another incident. On Good Friday in 1945, I was a thirteen-year-old Hitler Youth in a black SS uniform in a foxhole near Hungary. We were called the Werewolves, and we were trained to fight the Russians by doing underground work—destroying tanks and bridges and the enemies, the Russians. I knew I was going to die that day—because there was no chance to survive. There were 250 of us and there were 18,000 Russians who wiped out everybody in their way. So I gave the order to desert, which was against any other order, and all but five of my boys left. They all got killed. I survived. I could no longer endure any day after Good Friday for the nonsensical operation of a man called Adolf Hitler. That was the end of an old era—and the stepping out of that foxhole was the beginning of a new life. And ever since then I have been grateful for any Good Friday.

But behind that is the liberating deed of Jesus. And in that sense we all stand under His Cross still today, looking at Him for that promise of freedom. And the promise has been given; the promise has been heard; the promise has been experienced. And for this we give thanks, because it is the Good News—what we call the Gospel! Amen.

ᵱ

Reflections on the First Word

- Reflect upon Dr. Gritsch's thought about *the steps of baptism*:

  No, then *yes*, and finally—the "gift."

- Reflect upon Dr. Gritsch's statement, "the pastor—or those who baptize."

- Would you agree with Martin Luther when he called Good Friday the greatest holiday in Christendom? Why or why not?

- Since Jesus liberated us on the Cross on Good Friday, how are we called to live out this freedom in the twenty-first century?

- Reflect upon a time when you forgave someone who caused you mental, emotional, or physical anguish.

- Reflect upon the ramifications of being freed through the act of forgiveness.

THE SECOND WORD

"Truly I tell you, today you will be with me in Paradise."
—Luke 23:43

Conversations on death row are always honest. Before people die they usually do not lie anymore. They speak the truth. There is Jesus, surrounded by two criminals who probably deserved their punishment according to that law at that time. One goes on being the criminal—mocking Jesus. But the other one is honest and wants to be with Jesus. And so he is made the promise, "You will be with Me in Paradise today."

We always wrestle for honesty in the Church and in the world. We often pretend. We have conversations that are not always that deep. But when the time comes when a loved one has to leave us to die, and we have time to talk, talk is honest and no longer cheap. We have remembered that. In many churches we remember that death-row conversation on the Cross. In many churches the second word is made into a hymn. This song is sung during Holy Communion, quite often in Roman Catholic churches, but in some Lutheran and other churches. It is a song of hope as well as forgiveness. There is hope that that future which is promised, and is based on forgiveness, will really come.

Martin Luther's most favorite passage about hope was in the letter to the Hebrews, in chapter 11:1 where this writer says, "Faith is the assurance of things hoped for, the conviction of things not seen." Or as Paul put it, we see through a glass darkly and then we will see for real. The future with Christ begins with His forgiveness and with our hope.

People without hope are often clinically ill. One has to have hope. One has to have expectations. One has to have the assurance of some acceptance, some sign of love, some relationship—otherwise one becomes mentally a desert or dies. We live by hope. Our faith leads to hope, and we live by faith, hope, and love. We do this because we know that without that hope, things become worse. We are children of the Serpent. That famous Serpent in Genesis comes to the first people, Adam and Eve, and tempts them by saying, "Don't you want to be in charge of things? Don't you want to have the fruit from the tree of knowledge? Don't you want to live forever? Don't you want to be like God?" And when they answer in the affirmative, sin begins.

The world's original sin is the takeover game—the game of one human being taking over another. The world's original sin is the violation of the first commandment: "I am your God. Have no other gods beside Me." That is what is violated. And human beings, all of us, given the chance, love to dominate. We like to tell others what to do. We like to be told what to do. It is done in economics, in religion, in culture, in politics. There has never been a world without tyranny, whether it is in politics or family life, in marriage, in friendship, in the Church—there is always the temptation not to have dialogue, not to relate, but just to give ultimatums—to tell people what to do and what not to do. It is an easy way to live, but that is a world without faith, without forgiveness, without hope. The sin of the Serpent has been changed. The sin has been stepped upon on Good Friday.

There is a new life beginning. And ever since that Friday we are people who live between the times—the old times of sin where this game is still played, very seriously, and the new time that has broken in for those who already believe in that Jesus, and know and hope that He is going to come again. This new time no longer has the historical, Jewish, Messiah-looking king, but is the Son of God in all the glory. There will be a second coming!

And we are people between the first and second coming. We are the people of the meantime—of the interim between the ascension of Christ and when He comes again. Sometimes this meantime is a mean time, a miserable time. One might have to suffer. Sometimes it is a glorious time, but it is always an in-between time. We no longer really have a permanent residence. We are people of the Way, as the Bible puts it. We are pilgrims, sojourners, strangers, "resident aliens" (as one theologian puts it), ambassadors for Christ. We are always on the move—the people of the meantime who are the Church.

In his *Large Catechism*, on the Church, Martin Luther says that we are halfway on the way to heaven. There is still the old that we have to put down. There is still a tremendous need for forgiveness. But there is also the overwhelming hope that we will make it to Paradise. We know that we will go where Jesus is because no matter how criminal, the promise is there—when it is made by Him to us. There is no sin that might prevent it. Oh yes, we may have to repent, but we are on the Way. We are people of the Way!

But what do we do in the meantime? In that meantime we have a vocation. We have a job to do. We have to witness to this world that it is changing; the old is dying and the new is rising. We have a ministry to do, and that is why we organize in the Church. The only reason we exist as Christians is for mission, for ministry, for witness.

That is what all our education is about. That is what all our worship is about. That is what we call Christian formation. This means to be formed, to march in formation, to sing the hymns in formation, and to give the world an example of what it might be like if this world no longer wins. If sin actually is on the way out, and if people can love without boundaries—be they ethnic or national or whatever—then Christians are on the way to some form of universal love, faith, and hope.

Christian education and Christian worship have been for Lutherans the traditional two ways to be formed, to be nurtured for this mission. Luther reformed first the worship services in Wittenberg, and then he wrote the catechisms, and then he got the people together and told them that they all are ministers of the Word of God both as law that makes demands and as Gospel that makes promises. That is how the Lutheran movement was born and has survived to this day. If we do not do the job right in those two areas, Christian education and worship, we will not survive, and other movements will take over, because Lutheranism is not a church. It is a reform movement that shows others how it is to be done. We used to be the tough ones and sometimes still are!

We remember Bonhoeffer again today. He died on this day. There was a doctor in the concentration camp in Flossenbürg who saw this young unknown Lutheran pastor bound on a chair just before he was supposed to go to the gallows to be hanged. He was praying. He heard Bonhoeffer say, when he moved up the ladder to the gallows, "Life has just begun." To him this was the future. The old was already gone and he now lived by hope alone, by forgiveness alone, by faith alone. That is something on this side of the Cross that we have to remember. Even the criminal can say, "Jesus, remember me when you come into your kingdom."

And he will hear the answer, "Today you shall be with me in Paradise." All of us under the Cross have this promise. This is Good News, and that is the Gospel! Amen

Reflections on the Second Word

- Describe your ability to hope as you are confronted with the tragedy, rage, and violence in our current society, and answer this question: Is the Church a source of hope for you today? Why or why not?

- How do you define *original sin*? How does it impact your daily living?

- Reflect upon Dr. Gritsch's term "the mean meantime."

- In light of Martin Luther's statement about our being halfway to heaven, how would you characterize the "People of the Way"?

- Reflect upon Lutheranism as a reform movement as you consider Christian formation.

THE THIRD WORD

"Woman, here is your son . . . Here is your mother."

—John 19:26, 27

The scene under the Cross changes. There are two worlds: the soldiers and the women. The soldiers represent that old world, the way the world behaves: dividing the clothes, haggling about what is left from the dead. The world will do its thing about the remainders of a life. This is all according to Scripture. The soldiers do this as predicted in Psalm 22. In the Old Testament it was stated that this would happen to the Son of God. The drama goes on.

But there is a new world under the Cross: the women (Mary, her sister, Mary Magdalene) and the Beloved Disciple (some say that this was John who wrote the Gospel), the one Jesus loved particularly, who may have come late into his discipleship. Be that as it may, there is a new world that is pronounced under the Cross by the dying Jesus: "Behold your son! Behold your mother!" Blood no longer counts; family relationships are transcended. Faith creates new relationships that go beyond blood and beyond the bonds of family and tribe and nation—beyond the things that go on in this world. It happens in the midst of all the soldiers, who do not really understand. That is why they do not know what happened.

The Bible says that Israel was the real child of God and we Christians are the adopted sons and daughters. They are the first people of God, by blood and election, by history. We are the adopted children of God—just as we were adopted under the Cross, just as John became the new son in this world of the new mother Mary. What makes Mary special is that she experienced this new world from the very beginning.

We Lutherans sometimes have problems with the veneration of Mary, or the kind of saint she was, the kind of person she represents. But Martin Luther was very clear about it in his day. He said Mary is really the embodiment, the symbol of God's unmerited grace, of the way in which God's graciousness really works. He sometimes puts things upside down. He takes a pregnant, almost unmarried teenager and makes her the Mother of God. It blew Joseph's mind—as it did many in the world. This is not the way we see our children grow up. This is not the way a son or a daughter is born. But that Son was born of a Virgin. That Son was born of that kind of Mary whom God picked and selected. And Mary therefore for all times stood as the symbol of the Church, the Church that is adopted by the God of Israel, the Church that is pregnant with the Word, the Church that has to deliver, sometimes under the Cross, and in the midst of suffering, in the midst of the turmoil in this world. That promise is made, "Behold your son. Behold your mother."

Mary is that symbol, that expression of that new adoption, of that life that goes beyond family and beyond what we generally know. That does not mean that we should not honor family or blood and nation. It means that there is another world that has broken into our life, a future that has begun. We always go back to that future, back to that which our baptism promised us: that the Spirit will create a new world and we are on the Way. And John and Mary are the first of those symbols, the first of these bodies that are adopted.

Our saint for the day—Dietrich Bonhoeffer, the German Lutheran pastor that was killed on April 9, 1945—formed an interesting phrase about this new life. He called it "the cost of discipleship." He called it a way in which we must leave our favorite places and go to new places. He used as an example the Apostle Peter. There was Peter: with a good job as a fisherman, on a lake, with a good income, with friends—kind of incorporated into his job. And, Jesus says, "Peter, follow Me." Peter has to leave his boat; he has to become a landlubber. He has to leave; he is compelled to leave—not that he liked it, but he goes. If Peter had a chance to drive a car with a boat behind it, he would put on his bumper a sticker stating, "I'd rather go fishing!" instead of being that disciple, because it was a different life—totally different. And, he let the Lord know it; he was always the one who sometimes doubted and revolted, even betrayed Him just before the crucifixion.

In the Gospel of John, Jesus comes back to Peter from the resurrection, and says, "Peter, do you love me?" Three times He asked the question, because Peter was slow about these things. He did not get the point as quickly as others. He asked because Peter was stubborn; he loved this world; he loved his job; he loved his boat. Jesus asked the question because to leave one's favorite place, the place of security, sometimes one's family, is always very difficult. But that is the "cost of discipleship," of following, says Bonhoeffer.

He also calls it "costly grace." Grace has a price. And the price is to leave some things behind. If we do not leave what we love behind, Bonhoeffer says, then grace is no longer costly. It is cheap! Cheap grace means that we "ape" things. We say we believe in God. We do go to church, but we do not mean it. We follow rituals that have no meanings. We live a life of pretention. Bonhoeffer thinks that is what the German Lutherans did in his time. They pretended to be Christians and at the same time followed Adolf Hitler in great hoards, led by Lutheran pastors, 75 percent of them. They all signed an oath of allegiance—first Hitler, then Jesus. That was their confession. And Bonhoeffer went the other way, like Peter, but it was tough and he paid for it because grace was costly. It cost him his life, just as it cost Jesus His life when He made His kind of moves in the Israel of old. And so we remember that there is a life beyond the one we know—beyond family and blood and nation, beyond culture and all that we know.

I once, in 1971, was foster parent to a daughter fourteen years old who was on drugs and wanted a new life, and she could not do it. And the only way to do it was to be tough in love, to cut off the supply. So I became a Narc—joined the Lancaster State Police, arrested people in Gettysburg, bought from them all the drugs, until she was dried up and could not buy any more. But it was costly—some people said they were going to kill me. Others were saying they were going to burn down my house. But somehow one wrests one's way through to that word below the Cross, "Behold, this is your daughter!" Behold, things are new. They go beyond the traditional family sometimes. One should not always volunteer for these things, because the call is not always voluntary. You may be drawn into it.

The promises of God are very attractive and compelling, and love is then tough and no longer romantic, and things do not work as well as they used to. Under the Cross that new relationship has begun. The early Christians called it *agape*, love that is no longer selfish; *agape*, a love for others and not the love for self. And in that sense, the new life, the adopted life that God adopted for us, has begun. And that is good news! Amen.

Reflections on the Third Word

- How do you view Mary, the mother of Jesus?

- Reflect upon the statement "Faith creates new relationships."

- Dr. Gritsch talks about "going back to the future." What does this mean to you?

- Reflect upon the "cost of discipleship."

- Reflect upon the difference between the ideas of "costly grace" and "cheap grace."

THE FOURTH WORD

"My God, my God, why have you forsaken me?"

—Mark 15:34

When Martin Luther was a young man, even a child, he was trained very well what to do in emergencies. We would say he knew how to dial 911. In his time there was no 911, but you would dial a saint who stood by and helped. The saint of Luther's family was St. Anne, the mother of Mary, the grandmother of Jesus—a safe, reliable 911. And when he was in trouble, that is what he did. The last time, and the worst time when he was in trouble as a young man, was on his way home during a thunderstorm. As the story goes (and it is true), he got scared and he dialed and said, "Help, St. Anne! And if you do, I become a monk!"

And she did, and he did.

He was called to be a professor of Bible, and he pondered this question when he came upon Psalm 22. He got stuck on Psalm 22—almost for life. Even when he was married and his life became happier, he once asked Katie, his wife, "Why do you think that Jesus, of all people, prayed on the Cross, why? 'My God, My God, why have you forsaken me?' Why would Jesus who is God—the way we learned in school—why would He have to pray like that? Of all people, why should He be forsaken?" And Katie said, "Don't you know, Martin? He was one of us. He was human! That is why He prayed."

And so Luther always insisted on the humanity of God on the Cross. As silly as it sounds about a god (gods do not join this world—not the Greek gods, not the Roman gods, not the old gods), they do not become human. They do not become incarnate; they do not join the flesh; they stay where they are or they appear in certain forms, but they do not suffer. They are not like Jesus on the Cross. And so the Cross, or the "theology of the Cross," the message of the Cross, flies in the face of human reason most of the time. Although people who suffer badly, who are totally forsaken, they do know that help comes through suffering.

There is a psychiatrist who was my instructor in Vienna, Viktor Frankl, who wrote a book entitled *Man's Search for Meaning*. He developed a system called logotherapy that says that you survive only with a religious conviction. Only if something religious is in your head will you be able to stand up against all odds and say, "I want to live; because I have hope"—whether this is Buddhist, Jewish, Christian or whatever religion. He interviewed all the survivors he could lay his hands on—the Holocaust survivors among Jews in Germany, prisoners of war in Vietnam, and others—whoever had to survive. The evidence was always the same. They told him that at the worst time they could talk in a way that asked, "Am I forsaken?" And the answer was, "I'm not. I'm upheld." You cannot really be trained for this. It has to be given to you at decisive moments in life, the way a Bible verse might function after Confirmation, or what my grandmother told me as a Christian, or whatever that would be, that is the source of this. There is a 911 that helps us survive.

Jesus prayed, "Why have you forsaken me?" And He was not forsaken. And so we live with a God who is in solidarity with us, who is like one of us. The oldest version about Jesus is in the letter to the Philippians where it says there in chapter 2 verse 5 that Jesus came down from heaven like a god, but did not mind doing that. He emptied Himself for our sake, emptied Himself of all the glory and in this way joined us—became one of us, shared our doubts, shared our hopes and our fears, and our dreams—and since He has done that, we do not have to go through that anymore the way He did. He really substituted for us. He was a scapegoat; He stood in for us. He was, as some people say, the deputy for us, the defense attorney against evil—many names for that. He was the One who showed us a God who is like us, the humanity of God, the Crucified God, the God who comes as a Baby in Bethlehem and dies on a Cross at the place called The Skull—Golgotha—outside of Jerusalem. And so, whenever people are forgotten and when they are in trouble, they can identify with Jesus.

Our friend, Bonhoeffer, again, when he was imprisoned by the Germans, before his execution, he wrote a poem that was simply entitled, "Who Am I?" He said, "They say I am a strong pastor. I do my exercises. I am cheerful. That is my outward appearance, but I really feel forsaken. I really am close to suicide sometimes. But then I think of the God who came in Jesus, also to my cell in Berlin, and I know that I am His, and it is no longer my life, but my life in Him. Who am I?" He closed the poem, "I am the one, Lord, who is Yours. I am Yours." And then he could face the conspiracy and the persecution and his own cross, the mocking and the world and all the kind of stuff that is going on and the loneliness of dying—of dying alone.

There is something about being forsaken in the positive sense. We sometimes are put through this to reach the bottom line, to find out that sometimes we have to exist upside down, the way in which the teacher in the film *The Dead Poets Society* puts it: sometimes you have to jump on the table and teach and not do it the traditional way.

Sometimes the Christian faith has been compared to the invention of the supersonic jet. The story goes that the British tried to develop this jet and it had to be an airplane that flew beyond Mach 1, namely, faster than the speed of sound. They did not have a plane like that, with engines like that. So they asked for volunteers to dive in such a way that the speed so increased that they could break through the sound barrier where the airflow is reversed and you break through and it makes this thunderous sound. There was this one RAF pilot who said, "So many of my colleagues have crashed in the experiment because in the old planes when you put down the stick, you went down. When you pushed it up, you went up." And every time, just before the pilot crashed, he put the stick back, and instead of going up, he went down because the airflow was reversed, and he crashed. So that crazy mind—that one pilot said, "The heck with it! Just when I am about to crash, let's push it all the way down!"—and up he went! All they needed to do was build a machine that could reverse automatically the equipment so that the airflow could be forward and backward— that they could break through. But it took a mind that was almost inhuman and went beyond all human expectations, forsook everything that he was taught as an engineer about airplanes and airflows and science. It began to work because of his hunch and this last-minute, last-second desire, "Oh, why not?" And up he went!

Christians often fly with reversed controls. We break the sound barrier.

Precisely when we are forsaken—we are not! Some-one will show up! Nine-one-one works! It may not be St.

Anne; it may be a neighbor! Hold on to the people you know because you never know who they are. The Church will always provide such people—not in great numbers, but there is always a holy remnant. There will be one in whom Jesus is embodied, who will say, "You are not forsaken. You live My life with Me! You don't have to suffer just your loneliness; your homelessness is over and you have found a neighborhood!"

If the Church, somewhere along the line, could be such a place—a sanctuary for the forsaken, it would do its minimum mission in the world of at least being in solidarity with those who suffer; because that is the beginning of faith, hope, and love. So from that perspective—to be forsaken with Jesus—is a way up, a way out, a way to see the bottom line and not be hooked to it. It is a way of prayer. Besides forgiveness and hope and faith and love, there is prayer. Prayer works! One can talk to that God in straightforward human ways.

I was just in California in February, and everyone was complaining about the rain. For six years they complained about the drought. And for six years every Christian they could lay their hands on prayed for rain. Then they got it, and Governor Wilson climbed up on a ladder above the flood and said, "The drought is over." I heard some Christians say, "Maybe we shouldn't have prayed so hard. Maybe it was too much." Well, God is always rich in His grace. God is abundant, as is life. Eternal life is as abundant as this life. Look at the flowers; look at the trees; look what human beings can do in the arts and science when their imagination is really on.

Our brains have not even begun to function right. Haven't you seen that son of a Jewish rabbi on television who lost two-thirds of his brain in a car accident, and with one-third of a brain he went to Harvard and graduated *summa cum laude* and then went on television and said, "You only need a third of a brain to do this at Harvard." Harvard did not like him for that statement because they thought their students used all their brains. You can do it with a third and maybe less.

Human life under God is tremendously rich and powerful if we give it a chance—if we let go, if we yield our power to God's power. Faith is yielding power. Prayer is the way to yielding power. Prayer is the way to receive, to move back, to let my life be invaded by the world that has begun in my baptism. Prayer is the way in which the church breathes and gets its new life: in the intercessions for others, in the cry of loneliness. "Why my God, have you forsaken me?" The answer is, "I have not. I have not forsaken you. You think you have been forsaken. Stop thinking that. Yield, just yield, and in the yielding you will find help."

So under that Cross there is the memory of God. There is a loss of memory of that God. We have often lost that memory about the God that really joined us. We want a god who is like the usual god out there doing interesting things, like miracles and so on, but never invading our lives through people. And God always does that; because, there is a cross—usually also for us—and when we are on it we may say, "Why? Why God, have you forsaken me?" It is a fair question. It is a desperate question. It is a question we should ask. But, when it is asked, the answer is given, "I have not forsaken you!" Just look at your poor neighbor and you will find a little Christ who can help you.

Luther used to say every believing neighbor can be a little Christ for you, can be the Good Samaritan. And in that sense it takes two to believe, not one. Faith, by definition, takes two. It takes two to dance; it takes two to laugh—two to do the dance of the Gospel. It takes two to believe. It only takes one to die. But as long as we live, there are always two or three. And that is the good news! Amen.

❧

Reflections on the Fourth Word

- Can you name a religious conviction that you hold that is your 911? Can you recall a time that you relied on it?

- Have you ever wondered why Jesus thought He had been forsaken? What do you think of Katie Luther's reasoning?

- Do you really think of Jesus as being fully human? Just what are the ramifications of that fact?

- Why is it so difficult to see prayer as "yielding power," as Dr. Gritsch calls it?

- We often think of faith as a solitary act; therefore why do you think it takes two to believe?

THE FIFTH WORD

"I am thirsty."

—John 19:28

One of the last things people who die often do is eat or drink. There is a tradition about Roman crucifixions that that is expected, and sometimes the drink is pain killing or in some strange way refreshing. Jesus was given hyssop with wine. Hyssop is a mint herb that may produce peculiar tastes when mixed with Israeli wine. It was His last physical act. It is what His body needed because one dies on the cross of asphyxiation, of total paralysis, of all the body functions coming to an end—not of a loss of blood, not of a heart attack; gradually, everything dies. Asphyxiation. And again according to Scripture, that is what the Messiah has come to do. Even the drinking was prophesied by the ancient prophets.

Jesus Himself instituted a final meal before He left for the Garden of Gethsemane. It was called the Last Supper, and later the Lord's Supper and then the Supper of Thanksgiving, Eucharist—many names. Luther calls it the "Last Will and Testament of Jesus." That is why we do it. But when He said, "Do this," we do it, even if we do not always understand it. There have been many quarrels about that last meal when there should not be—about last things. One should just do it the way it was meant to be. One should teach it the way it is supposed to be done, not the way it is supposed to be understood in some odd, rational way.

There are two ways of talking about final things. One can describe them and be very clinical about it. One can be very medical, describing what happens. Twelve-year-olds and thirteen-year-olds always ask this question. When I taught confirmands as an interim pastor recently, a twelve-year-old said, "What did Jesus die of?" I said, "Well, what did you learn?" He said, "No one ever answered this question for me. I had all kinds of Sunday school teachers, but they did not give me a medical certificate. What would my father, who is a physician, write on this?" And I said, "Asphyxiation." And he said, "Aha, that's the answer." He just checked me out. He had asked his father before.

That is descriptive speaking about final things—cold-blooded talk that a neurosurgeon or a physician or a funeral director might use. There is another way to talk about final things, and that is declaring something, praising something, talking out of a relationship—like saying, "I love you"—and I do not describe it. We distinguish between this declarative speech and this descriptive speech and we often get confused, because at some odd moments there are some people who want to talk about final things the way they should be described when the other partner just wants to be told what to believe. That cannot be described. You declare something. You announce something. You herald something, and it is taken for that. You describe something, write up something, and the mind might grasp it in some way. These are two ways. But when someone says, "I am thirsty," one does not analyze; one gives a drink. When someone says, "I need help"—real help—one helps; one does not analyze.

There is a modern version about the Good Samaritan. The Good Samaritan sees the victim on the road and checks it out and does all the right things and really helps him physically. Well, the new version of this Samaritan, my seminarians tell me, is that someone goes by there and sees the victim and says, "Well, whoever did this to you needs a lot of help." Whoever did this to you needs a lot of help! And no one is helped. This is an interesting descriptive remark that does not establish a relationship. When someone says, "I thirst. I need help," you give him or her something to drink! Like Jesus—who was thirsty—and like all of us who need sustenance.

Jesus provided for His people after His death by saying, "I will be with you until the end of the earth. I will be with you in the Holy Spirit, whom I call the Paraclete, your Defense Attorney, the Advocate, who might even tell you what to say when you are in trouble. You will never be alone, when you do certain things, when you listen to My Word—to a new Word that says, from now on love each other. From now on it is the Golden Rule—love your neighbor as yourself—that at least will cancel your ego. At least that is 50 percent. At least it is justice; at least it is balance. But also, I sustain you in My presence, even physically through a Meal."

Because the God who has come to us is not just someone who is heard or sort of perceived in some nonhuman way. This God comes as food, this God comes as a baby. Martin Luther hammered this into his own church in his own day, which was so careful about it and so esoteric and so guarded about it. Only priests could handle the Holy Food, said the Church in AD 1215. You have to be seven years old before you go to the Eucharist, said the same Church. You laypeople do not understand what is going on; therefore, you cannot even touch the bread, the Host, at the Holy Meal. It must be given into your mouth. And drinking? You cannot drink at all! Only priests can do that! Of course this has been changed since (courtesy of Martin Luther, among other things). He said that we all are priests when we are baptized. We all drink. And when I say, "I am thirsty," I do not want to see someone else drink. I need that cup myself. I need to hold it and grab it and taste it. Luther said, "When I am in trouble, when I begin to lose my faith because my mind fools me"—theologians get fooled all the time—"when I am fooled, I want to eat God. I want to be so sure that I believe with my mouth by chewing, by eating, by tasting; because, sometimes faith is reduced to this simple act like the faith of a baby." When you want to have that baby more secure and in a real doxological position, you stuff something into its mouth, and sometimes the baby smiles at you, as if it were love, and maybe it is. If you do not do that, nothing else may help. It has to be that physical—and in that sense we are thirsty; we need to be sustained.

Christians have always shied away from that because it is so crude to believe in a God Who wants to give you un-leavened Jewish bread and this sip of wine. After all, there could be too much alcohol in it. There could be all kinds of problems with it. The Presbyterian Church just did a study on Eucharistic practices on the Holy Communion—to what degree it is dangerous from a medical perspective. They made a simple discovery. What is dangerous about it is the finger of the presiding pastor who gives you the bread. It is not in the cup. It is not in the bread. It is not in the sharing. All bacteria that are medically discernible are on the finger. So in some churches, you break your own bread. You do not use hands if you want to be clinical. If you do not want to be that physical, you do not want to take chances with that meal. And that usually domesticates the God we believe in. That usually means we really do not trust that much. It comes down to those things that we dare to do physically.

God has a Body. God takes up space and time. God comes as a sacrament. When we are fed through the pres-ence of Christ, it is not just bread; it is not just wine; it is not just baptism water. It is more than that because He said, "Do it this way and I will be with you in a New Covenant, in a New Life, in a way you have not dreamed about yet." All through that simplicity, all through that command. Martin Luther said in his *Catechism*, "The only reason we really do the sacrament is because it is commanded. We had others who tried to understand it and so we confused them. We say God is not just in the bread; we say that He is 'in, with, and under' the bread—just to confuse the others who want to explain everything." Some things are not to be explained. Some things are not descriptive.

I know a couple where he always complained and said, "Why should I tell you I love you? I told you that on our wedding day. Aren't you happy about it?"

"No," she said, "I want to have it said every day."

But he said, "This is silly."

She responded, "But of course it is silly, but I need to hear it."

He wanted to be descriptive; she wanted to be doxological. He had to come around and understand that.

God is seen doxologically in praise, in wonder, in acceptance by faith. That does not mean that my intellect should be in the backseat—not at all. It will free me finally not to believe in a God whom I need to domesticate—in a God, Luther says, I can put in my pocket, or the god-of-the-gaps who always functions when I need Him—or Her. No, God wants to be present all the time in ordinary things—in water and in bread and in wine.

Why God wants to be Jewish is an interesting question. But when Jews thirst even in the final hour, they take hyssop and wine, and sometimes some other things that are very unusual for us. In that sense God comes in His own history in a particular defined way. Our sacramental life needs to be informed by that because we do need sustenance. We are thirsty. We are hungry for the kingdom of

God. Of course it is not just that Final Meal, but that is what gets us at least going, that is the C-ration of life, that is the least we have: a visible Word besides the one we speak and hear.

It is then in the sacramental eating that our thirst is quenched and our hunger is stilled. When Jesus said, "I am thirsty," He did it as a dying person. But when He came back as the Resurrected Lord of all time, He said, "When you thirst, you will have My Blood, and you will have My Body. As a matter of fact, you will be part of My Body and My Blood. You will be called the Body of Christ, an organism of which I am the Head." As St. Paul said, "Christ is the Head and you are all the rest of it." Some might be dirty fingernails and others are the neck. It is still the Body. It still functions like that. It needs sustenance. So we are in constant need of reshaping our life of sustenance, of being reformed and reshaped and refreshed all the time in the way Jesus meant it to be, returning to that root that He established, the way He did it in that Last Meal, in that final commandment.

Our martyr friend, Dietrich Bonhoeffer, whom we honor today, used to say that life in the Church has become so corrupt, so worldly, that we should withdraw from the world. We should be like the ancient Christians—go into the catacombs, go underground, practice what he called "arcane discipline," a secret discipline, because upstairs (so to speak) it is too profane. We have gotten mixed up with the world. We just want to do it our own way. So instead of bread and wine, we will just have Coke and chips, or pizza or whatever, because this is a consumer society. "No!" said Bonhoeffer. We have to return to a discipline even if it takes going underground to find out once again where our real nourishment is. The arcane discipline is always a challenge for us Christians, because what is not done in secret is often perverted.

So, when we are thirsty, we know that Jesus is the Water of Life. Our baptism reminds us of that in our baptismal certificate. Our worship services give us the sustaining sacrament called the Eucharist. Luther says in his *Large Catechism*, "If you think you do not need it too often, just grab yourself by the chest and find out who you are—a miserable sinner. You should then run to it. If you do not believe it that way, read the Bible. If not, ask your neighbor how hungry you can get." But it is, quote, "The daily food."

The Lutheran Catechism is our normative teaching, not just a situational document. We need the Eucharist frequently. That is the only reason why we do it as often as we can, and as often as Jesus said we should do it, because in it He is present, and in it—as we say in our worship service—is "the foretaste of the feast to come," when all thirst is quenched. I am thirsty, and Christ quenches my thirst, and when you are thirsty, He will quench yours. That is the good news! Amen.

ᴂ

Reflections on the Fifth Word

- Reflect upon the aspects of "declarative speech" and "descriptive speech." Try to give examples of each.

- Give examples of how analysis often leads to paralysis (a common phrase of Dr. Gritsch) in our twenty-first-century world.

- Reflect upon the Holy Spirit as Advocate as you think

about the triune God.

- Why is it so difficult for us to accept that faith is often a very simple act?

- What do you think about when you consider sustenance? How does the Eucharist fit with these thoughts?

- What is the danger of a "domesticated God"?

THE SIXTH WORD

"It is finished."
—John 19:30

In a class where one learns Spanish, as I once tried to do in the beginners' class, the teacher sometimes takes the one who does not know Spanish very well, and says, "Why don't you finish the class by saying *Basta*"—which means "enough" or "stop"—"and then you can go home." You will not speak Spanish yet. It is just over until the next class.

When Jesus said, "It is finished," a new life began; it was not over. Ever since that time we have groups of Christians around the world, and especially in this country, who try in many ways to finish the work for Him. Some try to figure out the Last Days, when He is going to come again. They take their Scripture, and they take all the numbers in it, and they read the book of Daniel and the last chapters of Matthew and the book of Revelation. Then they say He might come in 1843 or in the year 2000. We have groups that are called Adventists because they are waiting for the Second Advent.

But in one way or another it cannot be said with certainty when Jesus will come to finish this world for real, and start the new one in a visible way. That is a burning question; the Gospels are saying in essence, He may come like a thief in the night. It could be tomorrow; so watch and pray and be ready. Live as if it would come now. Be responsible and obedient and faithful because you too have a witness to do that you finish in your life. You also have to finish something in this life that you began in your baptism, when you made promises in your confirmation when you said, "I will be a member of the Christian Church." Jesus said, "It is finished." Yes, but something new is going to come. There are those who think they have figured it out.

There is a second group that says, "Don't worry about it. Jesus is always with me, because I have His Spirit. I speak in tongues; I am joyful, and it is a wonderful life—a child-like experience of Jesus." And it is true. And it is beautiful to be a charismatic—that is, to have the gifts and the fruits of the Spirit. But sometimes you have to come down in this world and figure out how to witness with those who do not speak that language or are not like children.

I had a second foster daughter who spoke in tongues at age thirteen. Then she said, "What do you think of it?"

And I said, "Well, it is marvelous. You are a Christian baby. You do this nice baby talk every evening before you go to bed, but then in the morning you get up, and after school you come home with this young man called a date, and you behave like an adult, and you are only thirteen. I tell you what: why don't you be less a Christian baby and less of an adult being who likes so desperately to be thirty or forty or fifty as a woman and meet a man. Let's make a compromise: why don't you be just sixteen as a Christian and sixteen as a child?"

She was a bit puzzled by that. And I said, "You have three days to decide what you want to be—a Christian baby and at the same time an adult person who dates—but something has to give."

After three days she said, "Can I continue dating?" She never spoke in tongues again. It was tragic. She lost this aspect of babyhood.

There are people like that who say, "I have it all in my heart." And they do. They are as innocent as the doves, as Jesus says when He sends out His disciples. Be innocent as a dove. Do your cooing, but you know what happens to doves sometimes. Just when they love each other, they get shot down from the roof by some hunter or by someone who knows you can shoot doves when they love each other because then they do not guard each other. Most birds can be shot down that way.

That is why Jesus says, "When I send you out, I send you out like sheep among the wolves. Therefore, be as innocent as a dove, but as wise as a serpent." The serpent is not just the symbol of evil. The serpent is also the symbol of wisdom, of healing. Physicians have a symbol of the serpent on their sleeves in the hospital. It is healing power. One cannot always just practice servanthood as a Christian with the innocence of a dove—just saying that I love everyone and that I coo for everybody. No! You have to practice "serpenthood"—you have to be wise, and you have to wind your way through, and you have to give a witness where it counts. That takes brains and effort and dedication and imagination. It takes "detail work," as they say. Christians need to do detail work in this world: to be known and to out-think some others who do not think so well, to be kind in a way that we show the world what it really is: that it may not really succeed and that the end might come like a thief in the night. We have got to do our reality check with this world and with each other, even though we can still coo like a dove.

But we have got to move like serpents quite often. It is this world that is tough. Jesus died in this world for the one that is to come. And He suffered for that, and that means it is not yet totally over. The good life has not yet begun. Oh, it is here on a Sunday or when we assemble, or when we speak in tongues, or when we really are sort of together, but then there is Monday and Tuesday and Wednesday. As someone said, "Thank God there is Monday, because I have to go out and do things." There are those charismatics who ignore that, and there are those Adventists of all stripes who think the end should just come and get us out of here. There are people who are "born-again" in that sense. They say, I just want to be born-again once and that is it; it will last forever.

Luther says in his *Catechism*, "No, you have got to be born again daily." Every day you are born again and again and again. It is something that is going on and on and on until *you* are finished—not just Jesus. And so sometimes you have to do things that are not innocent, that are not like that of a baby, sometimes it is not just hymns and prayer and joy. Sometimes it is hard work to be a Christian. It is hard work to be an evangelist and a missionary. You have to learn other languages. You have to find out who your neighbors are, who they think they are, what reality is about. Sometimes you have to read newspapers and watch and listen to television to find out what it means to be a Christian today.

Again today we remember Bonhoeffer, the German martyr. He did the extraordinary thing by joining a spy system against Hitler—a military system that tried to assassinate this tyrant in Germany. They tried three times. They almost succeeded by 1944, but somehow they did not do it. When Bonhoeffer was asked, "Why do you do a thing like that as an ordained pastor, to be a counterespionage agent for the German Army?" he said, "Germany is driven by a driver who is mad—who sits behind the wheel and kills everybody. You cannot just stand in front of the car—you have got to kill the driver. You have to put the spoke in the wheel. You have to stop it. There is no ethical basis for that. There is no kind of reasonable answer for that. But that is the only way in which I can be a neighbor to my German people whom I love—to stop this man—through an act that no one can say is really ethical. It is beyond that. But I am called to do that."

And Bonhoeffer did, and he died for it. The conspirators almost succeeded, but then God took over, and history took over, and the Allies and the Russians and everyone else did Hitler in. But they tried—a spoke in the wheel, a serpent in serpenthood, not a dove: that sometimes finishes the job. It is a cruciform job. It is a job on the Cross, even for us—although never, never as hard as it was for Jesus. He did that for us, but we can rely on Him—when it gets tough, He is still tougher. When life gets tough, Christ gets going, not just we. He is the one who has overcome that.

And so we need in our calling in life something that we must finish, something that we must do that shows that we have a future to which He has called us. I used to go every year or so to East Germany when it was still a Communist country. It is the country of Martin Luther. Luther is my research object, so I went there. I took tours there, and I once went with a tour of people from Pennsylvania and California. We had the toughest tour guide ever—an East German Communist woman who was as tough as nails, who contradicted everything I said about Martin Luther, and falsified all of our Lutheran history—and she did it for ten long days.

After ten days we said farewell to each other. The way they do it in East Germany is that they take you to their fanciest hotel, which was built by the Japanese, has all the Western customs, and accepts only Western money. It is called the Hotel Merkur in Leipzig. The breakfast opens at 6:00 a.m., closes at 10:00 a.m., and the breakfast is a feast. The breakfast consists of shish kebob and frozen vodka and all kinds of things that you do not dream you want to eat for breakfast. For this woman this was just heaven! She had never seen things like this! For the first time she was

privileged to have this tremendous culinary feast, called a
Western breakfast in Communist eyes. She stayed in there
from 6:00 to 10:00 a.m. When she came out, she was almost
transformed.

She said to me, "You know, I may be a Communist
and you are an American, but we are all human beings. It is
just that your social system and your politics are not mine,
but underneath we are human beings. Why can't we understand each other?"

I said, "Miss So-and-So, you see this bus over there
with the Belgian license plate? We are going to leave in about
five minutes. And I am so glad to leave this country—your
miserable conditions, the reality that does not exist, even in
that hotel, the fact that you cannot speak the truth, and that
we cannot really dialogue. This is not just a difference in
systems; this is a basic issue of human freedom."

I thought she would strike me dead, because she
looked like it. She threw her arms around me and cried,
saying nothing, and I knew she wanted to be on that bus.
She wanted to leave. She knew what freedom was, and she
could not have it because no one had said to her, "For you
it is finished." It was not! She had to be stuck on that cross
called Communism and suffer for it for the wrong reasons
and we had a way out. That bus was the ticket to freedom,
just as my baptismal certificate is the ticket out of death and
the ticket out of this miserable life where I can say, "It is
finished." I do not have to endure it in the old way. Oh, it
may be here; it is like anxiety—you do not get rid of it, but
you contain it, and you domesticate it like a dog and say,
"Heel; sit; you're not going to be in charge." No depression,
no anxiety, no poverty will do it, because there was One
Man on the Cross who said, "I'm God, and it is finished for
you."

And in that sense we have to finish our lives. It is not
finished for us in one way. And it is finished in another way.

We are the interim people who have an assignment. We have to walk The Way—we have to go on that pilgrimage as strangers and sojourners on that bus to freedom. We are the freedom riders on that bus. We have known it for centuries. And Lutherans know it particularly well because they were originally oppressed by their own church. They know what it means to be betrayed by friends, and therefore we used to be tougher—and we still are. (That is why Lutherans used to be like the Doberman pinchers in the dog world.) They knew how to be tough and how to guard that Gospel, but also how to enjoy it and how to be innocent as a dove about it. Lutherans also know it takes "serpenthood" besides servanthood. And so, it is not finished for us, but we know there is an end in sight, and that is good news! Amen.

ॐ

Reflections on the Sixth Word

- If you knew that Jesus would be returning next week, what would you do to get ready?

- What does Dr. Gritsch mean when he talks of "servanthood" and "serpenthood," and how do these traits manifest themselves in your daily life?

- How would you define or describe "a cruciform job?"

- How do you recognize your calling, your vocation?

- Think about it being finished for you in one sense and at the same time it is not finished for you.

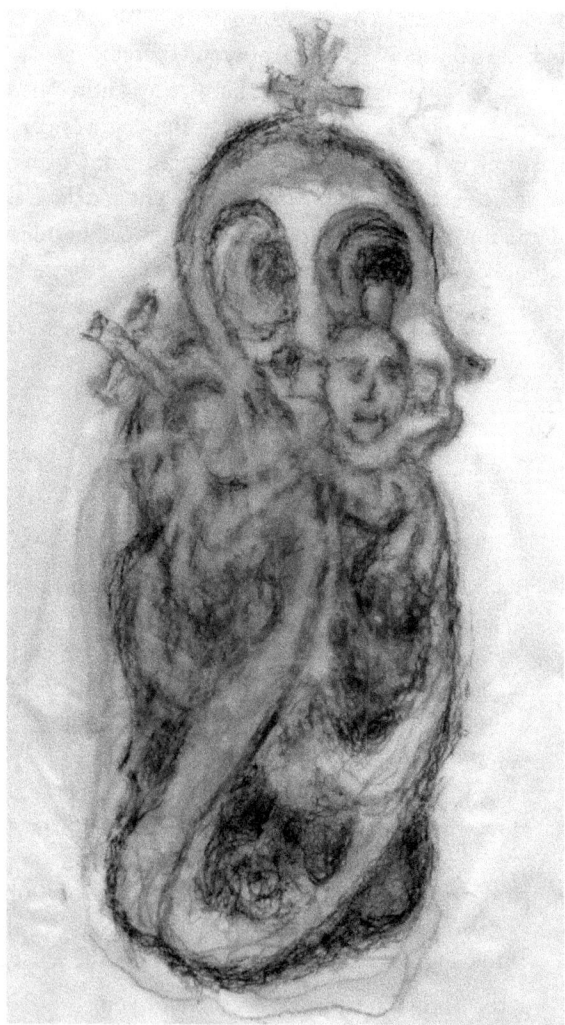

THE SEVENTH WORD

"Father, into your hands I commend my spirit."

—Luke 23:46

"Father, into your hands I commend my spirit." I never forget these words because on one day in 1980 in a 747 airplane flying from Washington DC to Frankfurt, Germany, near Halifax, Canada, the plane went down. It went from about forty thousand feet to five thousand feet in fifteen-sixteen seconds and then got out of it. I was sitting next to a young man who was reading a book, and when we went down, he began to pray the Lord's Prayer and then ended it very calmly by saying, "Father, into your hands I commend my spirit."

And there was I sitting saying, "Ah, when am I going to finish my Luther book?" I did all the things that people say when you are about die. You want to finish things. You are egotistic. You want to do your thing.

Since I spent the next twenty-six hours with this young man, I discovered he was a former Catholic monk, who became a dogfighter pilot in the American Air Force and who was flying on assignment to Germany to his F-16, 18, 24—whatever. He had a discipline that was phenomenal—as a Roman Catholic Christian. And, he was a layman, and I was ordained! I was supposed to be the officer. He was supposed to be the layperson. And he beat me on every count in Christian discipline. He said what needs to be said when the chips are down, and when an airplane goes down. And, he was saved.

It takes formation. It takes that discipline to live in this life because it is surrounded by problems—deep ones that one cannot escape. One has to go through them, not around them. Martin Luther said that what makes a good Christian and theologian is suffering. Not that you can avoid it, but you go through it with that hope and faith and love that we learned from Christ, who bequeathed it to us in His Word and Sacrament.

So all of life is, in that sense, in the hand of God, and that is the only commendation it has. We use that word, *to commend*, usually when we bury people. "We commend you now," we say in our funeral liturgy. We commend you now to God. But life was already commended at birth to that only place and way and Being to whom we can commend it—the God and Father of Jesus Christ. In essence, in substance, in what we live and die for, it is really that simple faith that we are in God's hands. He's got the whole world in His hands. And that is the simplicity and the beauty of our so-called religion.

Lutherans rediscovered that in the sixteenth century by saying that we live by faith alone, by Christ alone, by grace alone, even by the Word alone, by the Cross alone. We know what it means to be solely and uniquely and exclusively trained and focused on that Christ on the Cross, because in that Cross God loves even the ungodly—those who do not deserve it, those who have no merits whatsoever. But that faith needs to be experienced in community with others who enact it for us. Justification by grace, through faith, without works (as we say as Lutherans with St. Paul) is not just a doctrine. It is a liturgical experience. It is when the Word is said to me, and I believe it. It is enacted to me in the Sacrament and I can see it and taste it. That is when I experience the righteousness of God—to be right in His sight. That is when it happens—not just when I describe it. It happens when it is declared to me, when it becomes an event, a gathering, a happening that we call church when Christians do this with and to each other.

That is why to Luther and to Paul, Abraham in the Old Testament was the great example of faith. Abraham was asked to sacrifice his own son. The Danish theologian Søren Kierkegaard wrote about this in his book entitled *Fear and Trembling,* where he said, "All the morality in the world was suspended at that moment when Abraham was asked to kill Isaac; because, it was a test of faith." And just when he was about to do it, God told him to look behind a bush! There was a goat or an animal like that which he could sacrifice. Abraham did not have to sacrifice his own son. But, he had this faith—this unconditionally strong faith that can move mountains.

Our friend and martyr, Dietrich Bonhoeffer, ran a seminary, an underground seminary, in 1937 on some Baltic-German beach, secretly, because Hitler no longer allowed theological seminaries and divinity-school students. He trained about sixteen young men there. He told them that every day they should confess their sins to each other in private. Private confession was the order of the day, because you may be so close in Christian combat that you must trust each other, and no spark of doubt or distrust should be left in you because you may serve in this unconditional way, and for this you should be trained. Bonhoeffer then wrote a book about this called *Life Together,* in which he describes the discipline it takes to be so faithful and so full of grace that one can really trust the other teammate—whoever sits next to you in the airplane of life when it goes down—and who knows what to say and knows what to do. "Father, into your hands I commend my spirit." That is all that needs to be said. One should not say, "When do I finish my thing?"

It is faith in that Word and in that new life which has begun at Golgotha. That new life has Easter on the horizon with something that will be so new that it will almost blow us away.

Just recently Marian Anderson, the black singer, died. There was a time when we had problems with color and she had not been allowed to sing at the United Nations and elsewhere. It was at this time that she sang "He's Got the Whole World in His Hands." That is the simple truth; that is the one commendation; that is the one Gospel News that we need to hear—He's Got the Whole World in His Hands.

That is why we can say, "Father, I commend my spirit into your hands." That is almost Easter news, even on Good Friday. We remember, even today, that Easter is around the corner. We remember in our forsaken world that there is the rise of the Easter sun. And in that sense, we rededicate ourselves and commend ourselves all over again—in our worship, in our programs, and where we are in our specific calls and stations of life—because not we but He has the whole world in His hands. And therefore we commend our spirit to Him. And that is the Gospel! Amen.

Reflections on the Seventh Word

- Reflect on your own faith journey.

- Who/where are your faith partners?

- Reflect on your willingness or ability to "commend" *everything* to God.

- What role does Christian formation play in this act of commendation?

- Reflect upon the issue of suffering as it relates to your beliefs.

FINAL REFLECTION

We remember, even today, that Easter is around the corner. We remember in our forsaken world that there is the rise of the Easter sun. And in that sense, we rededicate ourselves and commend ourselves all over again.

- Reflect upon Good Friday's good news as we await the Easter sun which is just around the corner.